Myanmar

Myanmar

BY WIL MARA

Enchantment of the World™
Second Series

CHILDREN'S PRESS®

An Imprint of Scholastic Inc.

Frontispiece: **Temples and hills in Rakhine State**

Consultant: David I. Steinberg, Distinguished Professor of Asian Studies Emeritus, School of Foreign Service, Georgetown University, Washington, D.C.

Please note: All statistics are as up-to-date as possible at the time of publication.

Book production by The Design Lab

Library of Congress Cataloging-in-Publication Data
Mara, Wil.
 Myanmar / by Wil Mara.
   pages cm. — (Enchantment of the world)
 Includes bibliographical references and index.
 ISBN 978-0-531-23294-1 (library binding)
 1. Burma—Juvenile literature. I. Title.
 DS527.4.M37 2016
 959.1—dc23   2015021729

1 2 3 4 5 6 7 8 9 10 R 25 24 23 22 21 20 19 18 17 16

Shwezigon Temple, Pagan

Contents

Left to right: **Shan Plateau, rainy day, planting rice, fishing, family**

CHAPTER 1

Opening Up to the World

8

FIFTEEN-YEAR-OLD MYA IS WALKING WITH HER FRIENDS to school in Kalaymyo, a small town in northwestern Myanmar. She is dressed neatly in a pressed green skirt and white shirt. All of her friends are dressed the same, because wearing uniforms to school is required by the government. She likes school, although some subjects are more interesting to her than others. She doesn't complain about those she doesn't like, however. She knows that going to school is a privilege. Her parents remind her of that all the time. Some of her friends had to drop out of school because their families are so poor that everyone has to work just to make ends meet.

Mya has many dreams. One is to someday move to the city of Yangon, which is no longer Myanmar's capital but is still a bustling and vibrant place teeming with opportunity. She would like to meet a nice man one day, get married, and have children. But she would also like to have a career. Her school

Opposite: **Schoolchildren in Myanmar usually wear green and white uniforms.**

Myanmar or Burma?

The country of Myanmar has two names. In the past, it was officially called Burma. But in 1989, the nation's military government changed the name to Myanmar, a longtime written form of the name. Most of the world accepted that change. The United States and the United Kingdom, however, continue to use Burma. In this book, Myanmar is used for the modern period, and Burma is used for earlier times. The government also changed the name of some cities, geographic features, and other sites. For example, Rangoon, the nation's largest city, is now Yangon.

has a few computers, and she is fascinated by them. She is particularly fascinated by the Internet; the way you can be in contact with people on the other side of the world. Her parents never had anything like that. Her father has never even been to Yangon. Her mother was, once, and talks about it all the time. But they are farmers now, and they have worked long and hard to keep their household going. They want Mya to have a better life. They love to hear her talk about her dreams, of moving to Yangon and getting a job as a teacher. She wants to teach science, and she has a particular fondness for biology. She is fascinated by things that live and breathe and grow, and she wants to share that joy with others.

What worries Mya the most is when she hears her parents and other relatives talk about how they don't know what's going to happen with their government and their country from one day to the next. They have hopes that great things will be happening in their country. They hear of new oppor-

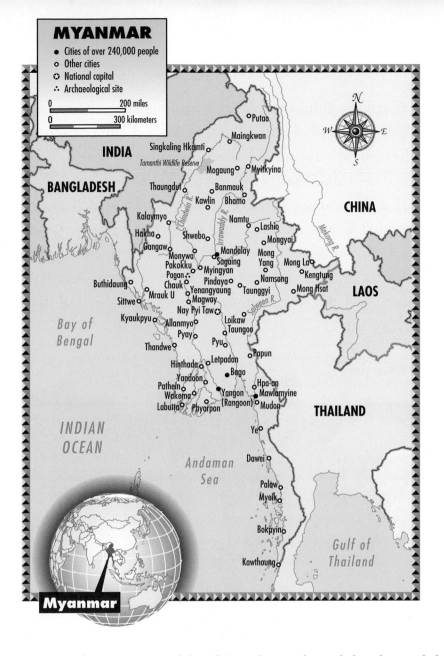

Myanmar

tunities for women, of freedom of speech and freedom of the press, of better working conditions for laborers of all kinds, of relationships for the first time between Myanmar and other countries. She still hears stories from her family about how the government was once run by the military. When she hears the word *military* she thinks of soldiers in camouflage uniforms and black leather boots holding rifles. It makes her shiver to think that the military controlled the government. "For a long, long time they did," her grandmother said to her once. And they ruled the country by force, Mya was told, which means if they didn't like something, they used their brute power to change it. Now, however, she is told that the government has been changing. Many reforms have been enacted. And that all sounds good, but when will these things actually start happening?

Rebel soldiers from the Karen ethnic group walk by children in a village. Karen groups have frequently fought to achieve greater independence from Myanmar.

People from Myanmar are usually called Burmese. Sometimes, however, they are referred to as Myanmese.

The forms of people's names in Myanmar are much different than forms used in other parts of the world. There are no family names, and every person has his or her own name that is used for life. Women do not change their names when they get married. When talking to someone, the full name is used. When Burmese people go overseas, however, they often have to take one of their names as a family name for passports.

Most Burmese people are not addressed as *Mr.*, *Miss*, or *Mrs.* Older respected men are called by the title *U*, which means "Uncle." Older respected women are called *Daw*, which means "Aunt." Family members are called by titles with meanings such as "elder sister" or "younger brother."

Mya thinks about all of these things as she gets ready for another day at school. She is a good student, and she's proud of that. She doesn't mind working hard. It makes her feel good about herself and good about the fact that she's building toward something. She's not sure what, though, and that bothers her all the time. There's so much uncertainty about what direction her country is heading in. What is our identity? Who controls our government? Until some of these questions are answered, it's hard for Mya to decide where she's going with her own life. She realizes she's living in a nation that is clearly moving in a new direction—but where?

No one knows for certain.

CHAPTER 2

The Lay of the Land

MYANMAR IS LOCATED IN SOUTHEAST ASIA. THE country is shaped something like a kite, or roughly that of a diamond, with a long tail hanging down in the southeast that is part of the Malay Peninsula. India and Bangladesh lie to the west of Myanmar, China to the northeast, and Laos and Thailand to the east. To the south and southwest are the Andaman Sea and the Bay of Bengal, which open into the Indian Ocean. Myanmar is the second-largest nation in Southeast Asia, trailing only Indonesia in size. It covers roughly 261,000 square miles (676,000 square kilometers), making it slightly smaller than the U.S. state of Texas.

Opposite: **Green mountains rise from the Shan Plateau in eastern Myanmar.**

Highlands and Lowlands

Myanmar's land can be divided into two main areas—the lowland region that runs north–south through the center of the nation, and the rugged mountains and other highlands that surround it. The lowland area is called the Central Valley, and it features Myanmar's two most prominent rivers—the Irrawaddy (also spelled Ayeyarwady) in the west and the Salween (Thanlwin) in the east. The Irrawaddy is the nation's largest waterway and serves as a critical route for commercial shipping and other travel. The Irrawaddy flows for about 1,350 miles (2,200 km), creating a broad and fertile delta area in the south before finally draining into the Andaman Sea.

Myanmar's towering mountain ranges run along its borders. The nation's highest point, called Mount Hkakabo, lies in the north and reaches an elevation of 19,296 feet (5,881

The entire length of the Irrawaddy River is in Myanmar. Boats can travel on most of its length.

meters). The highest point in all of Southeast Asia, it is part of the Himalayan chain of mountains, which includes the highest peaks in the world. The northern highlands boast Indawgyi Lake, one of the largest lakes in Southeast Asia.

The Rakhine (Arakan) Mountains run along Myanmar's southwestern border. They continue south, straight into the Bay of Bengal, where they eventually resurface in the form of some of Myanmar's outlying islands. The Patkai, Naga Hills, and Chin Hills separate Myanmar from India.

In the east, the Shan Plateau rises abruptly from the Central Valley. This flat region has an average height of about 3,000 feet (900 m). It connects to several hill regions, including the Karen, Tenasserim, and the Dawna. This series of ranges includes thickly forested river valleys and some wide stretches of flat plains. Much of this area is unpopulated, and it serves as a rich source of gems and other minerals.

Myanmar's Geographic Features

Area: About 261,000 square miles (676,000 sq km)

Highest Elevation: Mount Hkakabo, 19,296 feet (5,881 m)

Lowest Elevation: Sea level along the coast

Longest River: Irrawaddy, about 1,350 miles (2,200 km)

Longest Border: With Thailand, runs 1,501 miles (2,416 km)

Average High Temperature: In Yangon, 99°F (37°C) in April; 89°F (32°C) in October

Average Low Temperature: In Yangon, 76°F (24°C) in April; 76°F (24°C) in October

Average Annual Precipitation: In Yangon, 106 inches (269 cm)

Coolest Area: In the northern mountains, temperatures drop well below 32°F (0°C)

Hottest Area: In the central plains, temperatures can reach 113°F (45°C) during April

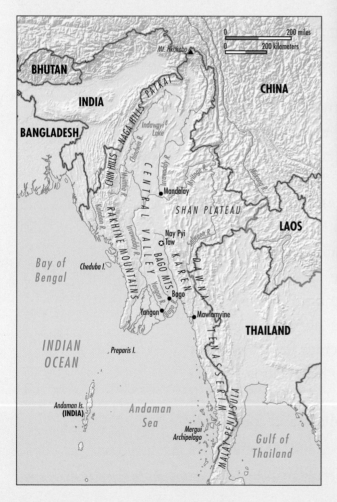

Myanmar lays claim to the Mergui Archipelago, which includes hundreds of islands off the southwestern coast. These islands feature sandy beaches, warm blue waters, thick forests, and idyllic fishing villages. Many were opened for tourism only in the last few decades, and some have become popular diving destinations.

Most of the small islands in the Mergui Archipelago are uninhabited.

Climate

Myanmar has three climatic seasons. Monsoon season occurs from late spring to early or mid-fall. The word *monsoon* refers to the strong winds that blow through much of southern Asia at different times of the year. During monsoon season, these winds blow in from the southwest, picking up moisture from over the sea. The cloudy skies of monsoon season bring heavy rains, with the total rainfall reaching as much as 200 inches

In much of Myanmar, July and August are the rainiest months.

(500 centimeters) in the upper regions of the country and about half that in the lower regions. The central areas, on the other hand, receive only about 30 inches (75 cm) of rain.

After monsoon season, the weather tends to cool off a bit from about November to February. This is followed by a hot season, which lasts a few months in mid-spring. Temperatures can top 100 degrees Fahrenheit (38 degrees Celsius) in some areas during this time, and in certain regions the lack of rain can produce extremely dry conditions. The higher areas of Myanmar are generally drier, while the lowlands, particularly along the coast, tend to be more humid. The northern mountains receive heavy snowfall in the winter.

Snowfall is common in Myanmar's northern mountains.

Looking at Myanmar's Largest Cities

Yangon (below and right), formerly known as Rangoon, is the largest city in Myanmar, with a population of around 4.5 million. It is located in the extreme south of the country, at the point where the Yangon and Bago Rivers meet. Yangon is the capital of the Yangon Region and served as the capital of Burma as a whole from the mid-1800s until 2005. Much of downtown Yangon consists of late nineteenth-century British colonial buildings. But the city's most prominent building is the Shwedagon Pagoda, a great Buddhist temple complex covered in gold that dominates the city's skyline. Yangon is the most diverse city in the nation, with large

numbers of people of Indian and Chinese descent as well as large populations of people from the Rakhine and Karen ethnic groups. Millions of people flocked to the city in the late twentieth century. It was a bustling center of economic activity for decades, offering opportunities for anyone looking to rise above the grind of the rural agricultural industry. Today, most of the governmental bodies have moved to the new capital city of Nay Pyi Taw, and Yangon has lost some of its appeal to newcomers. It remains, however, the nation's center of trade, industry, media, and tourism.

Mandalay (facing page, top), located in the center of the nation on the Irrawaddy River, is Myanmar's second-largest city, with a population of about 1.2

million people. The city was the last capital of the Burmese kingdom, serving as capital from the late 1850s until the British took control of the region in 1885. Today, Mandalay is the most important Buddhist center in Myanmar, with hundreds of monasteries and pagodas. It is also the main hub for economic activity in the northern half of the country, including trade with China and India.

The nation's third largest city is the capital, Nay Pyi Taw, with a population of about 925,000. Mawlamyine (right) is Myanmar's fourth-largest city, with a population of about 440,000. It sits at the northern end of the Malay Peninsula, at the mouth of the Salween River. Mawlamyine served as the British colonial capital of the region from 1826 to 1852. Mawlamyine has wide religious diversity, with a strong Buddhist presence as well as Christian and Hindu communities. The city is a major port and trading center. It is also noted for its excellent cuisine. In particular, it is noted for the huge variety of fruits available there.

CHAPTER 3

The Wild Side

MYANMAR HOSTS THOUSANDS OF ANIMAL species of all shapes and sizes. It has more than three hundred mammal species, another three hundred reptiles and amphibians, more than one hundred birds, and thousands of varieties of fish. Many species that live in Myanmar are endemic, meaning that they are found nowhere else in the world. Parts of the nation remain unstudied. Scientists are only now getting the chance to explore some of Myanmar's natural riches, and they are continually discovering species that have been unstudied and uncataloged for thousands of years.

Mammals

The largest mammal in Myanmar is the elephant. Asian elephants grow to a shoulder height of about 9 feet (2.7 m) and weigh up to 5 tons, with the females generally being a bit smaller than the males. Elephants in Myanmar can be found

Opposite: **A Bengal tiger cub peers through the grass. Only about three thousand tigers live in the wild throughout the world. A small number live in Myanmar.**

in a variety of habitats, most commonly open grasslands and forests. They only rarely venture into the high-elevation areas. They are remarkably intelligent and demonstrate a wide variety of emotions, aiding the injured and mourning the missing of their herds. They are visibly upset when herd members die and will often try to bury the dead. In Myanmar, elephants are sometimes used in the logging industry.

Myanmar is also home to many primates, including a variety of monkeys, gibbons, and macaques. One of the most widespread of these is the dusky leaf monkey. It is a little creature with a very

Elephants have long been used as work animals in Myanmar.

Dusky leaf monkeys are usually orange at birth but turn gray or brown as adults.

long tail. In fact, it is often called a *langur*, which means "long-tailed" in the Hindi language of India. It rarely weighs more than 20 pounds (9 kilograms). It can survive in a variety of habitats, but it prefers forested areas with plenty of leafy cover because it spends much of its time among the branches.

Many large cats make their homes in Myanmar. Tigers, leopards, clouded leopards, and wildcats all live there. They are all endangered, however, as their habitats are shrinking. They are also dying as a result of human activities such as hunting. In Myanmar, illegal hunting is a problem. Many tigers and other large cats are killed for their parts, such as the skin, the claws, and the teeth, which are prized items in China. Many of these animal parts are sold in the Burmese town of Mong La, near

Red pandas have thick fur over their entire bodies, including the soles of their feet. This helps keep them warm and keeps them from slipping on wet branches.

the Chinese border. Although much of this trade is illegal, the Burmese government has not yet stopped it.

Other large mammals that live in Myanmar include rhinoceroses and buffaloes. The country is home to the large Eld's deer and the small barking deer, and to red pandas. These adorable reddish-brown creatures, which have long, bushy tails and raccoon-like faces, spend most of the time in trees.

Tamanthi Wildlife Reserve

Located on the shores of the Chindwin River in a remote area of northern Myanmar, the Tamanthi Wildlife Reserve was established in 1974 to protect the rapidly vanishing Sumatran and Javan rhinoceroses. Though the rhinoceroses no longer survive in this area, it remains an ideal natural home for many rare species, including the Indochinese tiger, the white-winged duck, and the barking deer.

There are many smaller mammals throughout Myanmar, including hedgehogs, shrews, and moles, plus a broad range of rodents such as rats, mice, squirrels, and porcupines. Among the most interesting rodents in Myanmar are flying squirrels. These creatures cannot fly like birds do—by flapping wings and lifting off the ground. Instead, they leap from a branch or other high spot and sail through the air with the aid of a large flap of furry skin that stretches from their forearms to their back legs. Ten different species of flying squirrels live in Burmese forests.

A red giant flying squirrel sails through the air. It is one of the largest species of flying squirrels in Myanmar.

Myanmar is also home to about a hundred bat species. In fact, about one-fifth of all Burmese mammals are bats. Among the best known is the lesser false vampire bat. This species lives by the thousands in caves, tree holes, and abandoned buildings, and feeds during the night on whatever insects it can catch. It does not, in fact, attack humans and suck their blood, but it does carry diseases that can be harmful to people.

The waters off Myanmar also host mammal species, including whales, dolphins, and porpoises. One of the most impressive is the blue whale. Stretching an average of 100 feet

A blue whale brings its tail out of the water as it prepares to dive deep. Blue whales are so large that their tongues can weigh as much as an elephant.

(30 m) in length—about as long as two and a half school buses lined up—and weighing about 200 tons, the blue whale is the largest animal on earth. Aside from its remarkable size, it is a beautiful animal, with a blue-gray back and a lighter gray on its underside. Its main diet is krill—tiny creatures found in huge quantities in the ocean. The blue whale eats about 4 tons of krill every day.

The gray peacock-pheasant is a large bird, often about 2.5 feet (75 cm) long.

Bird Life

Birds are also plentiful in Myanmar; experts have identified more than one thousand different species in the nation. Ducks and geese, woodpeckers, ospreys, falcons, and eagles can all be found there. The hooded treepie lives only in Myanmar. A beautiful gray bird with a long black tail, it lives in the central part of the nation.

A bird long associated with Myanmar is the gray peacock-pheasant. This large bird is a beautiful gray color mottled with

shiny blue and sometimes green or purple spots ringed in both black and white. The gray peacock-pheasant lives in forested areas in lowland regions, where it feeds on fruits, seeds, and small bugs.

Myanmar is also home to the majestic black eagle, a fearsome predator that swoops down toward the treetops to snatch small mammals or bird eggs.

Reptiles and Amphibians

Roughly two hundred species of reptiles and amphibians are found in Myanmar. One of the largest is the reticulated python. The longest snake on earth, the average adult grows to about 15 feet (4.5 m) although some have reached 25 feet (7.6 m). The reticulated python inhabits a variety of environments—everywhere from rain forests to open grasslands—where it hunts mammals. Some smaller reticulated pythons might hunt rats, while large ones might make a meal of a deer or a pig. The snake swallows the prey whole, and sometimes does not need to eat again for months. Another noteworthy snake found in Myanmar is the fearsome king cobra. King cobras can reach 18 feet (5.5 m) in length, and they have a toxic bite that is often fatal.

Myanmar is also home to the world's largest land predator, the saltwater crocodile. Some of these ferocious creatures have reached 21 feet (6.4 m) in length. These crocodiles spend most

Reticulated pythons live a long time for snakes. In the wild, they have a life span of fifteen to twenty years. In zoos, they sometimes live twenty-five years.

of their time relaxing in the water. They are ambush hunters, gobbling up whatever comes near them in the water, including fish, wading birds, monkeys, and other mammals.

A large lizard called the water monitor is an excellent hunter, eating birds, fish, turtles, young crocodiles, mammals, and other creatures. Much less fearsome is Myanmar's tiny painted chorus frog, which grows less than 1 inch (2.5 cm) long. It lives in marshes, swamps, and thick forests, where it feeds on insects. Many reptiles and amphibians are endemic to Myanmar, including the Burmese star tortoise, the Toungoo frog, and the Burmese spitting cobra.

The Burmese star tortoise is endangered because of hunting. People in Myanmar have long eaten tortoise meat, but now even more of the tortoises are killed so that their beautiful shells can be sold in Europe or North America.

Plant Life

Myanmar boasts a wide variety of plants. The rain forests are a wealth of life and light, filled with evergreen trees, bamboo (which is actually a grass), vines, and flowers such as hibiscus and orchids. One of the most prominent tree species in the nation is teak, a large hardwood known for its toughness. In particular, it resists water damage, which makes it ideal for building things such as boats and bridges.

In the mountainous areas, the land is covered with deciduous trees and shrubs—those that tend to lose their leaves during the cooler times of the year. Along the coast, palm trees are common, as are mangrove trees, which can grow directly out of the salt water. Beautiful casuarina shrubs thrive along the edge of the sea. Casuarina wood is hardy and versatile, used for everything from building homes to burning firewood, and its fruit provides vital nutrition for local residents.

Casuarina trees can grow in the sandy ground along the sea.

Two Symbols

Two flowers are considered national symbols of Myanmar. The first is the thazin orchid, which produces beautiful white blooms in the late fall and is common to lowland forest regions. The delicate flower is a symbol of purity. It is said that during the Konbaung dynasty (1752–1885), the royal family had the right to the first thazin that bloomed each year. Only after the family got their thazin were commoners allowed to pick them and use them.

The other national flower is the bloom of the padauk (right), a small tree with oval leaves and golden yellow flowers. It is a tough tree, able to survive harsh weather and attacks by armies of termites. Its hardwood is used in the construction of furniture and toolmaking. The padauk and its flower represent youth, strength, and love, both for people and for the country of Myanmar.

Conservation Issues

Myanmar has a wealth of natural wonders. For a long time, the country was politically cut off from most of the rest of the world, and its isolation helped protect its environment. Sadly, however, the changes in the nation in recent years have taken a toll. Deforestation—the destruction of forests—has increased rapidly. From 1990 until 2010, nearly 30,000 square miles (78,000 sq km) of tree cover were lost. That's an area nearly the size of the U.S. state of South Carolina.

This deforestation has destroyed the habitat for thousands of species, wiping out populations that had thrived for centuries. The logging trade—both legal and illegal—has been partially responsible for this, as has the need of the growing human pop-

ulation to build homes and towns. Wetland areas—among the most fragile of ecosystems—have also come under assault from aggressive mining activities and the demand for more farmland.

Although the government of Myanmar has taken some steps to preserve its natural areas, those steps have often been too small or too laxly enforced to actually protect the land. Furthermore, as the Burmese population grows, so does the need for people to turn to the wild for their everyday needs of food, building materials, and ways to make a living. Conservation groups from Myanmar and elsewhere have begun addressing some of these problems, but progress is difficult. Myanmar remains a place rich in biodiversity—a place where many different species live. But unless action is taken to protect the land and the creatures that live there, that biodiversity will remain severely threatened.

Workers load wood onto boats at a logging camp on the Salween River in eastern Myanmar. The timber is taken to Thailand to be sold.

CHAPTER 4

A Long History

PEOPLE HAVE OCCUPIED THE LAND KNOWN TODAY AS Myanmar for hundreds of thousands of years. The earliest evidence of people in that area forming simple communities, making crude tools, domesticating animals, and growing their own food dates from around 11,000 BCE. In about 500 BCE, people in the region were using iron. By this point, the Burmese people were forming villages with increasingly complex social structures, making advancements in agricultural techniques, and beginning to trade goods with surrounding communities. There is also evidence to suggest that society was evolving a class structure, with wealthier and more privileged people enjoying greater luxuries than those in the lower ranks.

Opposite: **A stone lion stands in Halin, an ancient Pyu city.**

Early Kingdoms

Around 200 BCE, the Pyu people moved southward into the lowland areas of central Burma. At least five large city-states—independent cities, each ruling the area surrounding it—existed in the region at this time. Thick protective walls encircled the cities, and the people lived in wood houses with tin roofs. Pyu society continued to develop into the ninth century CE. The Pyu people irrigated fields to grow rice, formed basic governments, and adopted the Buddhist religion, which had emerged in what is now India and spread eastward. They also engaged in widespread trade and used silver coins.

These sculptures made by the Pyu date to the sixth or seventh century CE.

The Mon people lived south of the Pyu, in lower Burma, as well as in what are now Thailand and Laos. The Mons' major city in Burma was Thaton, at the mouth of the Salween River. Thaton was established sometime around the fourth century BCE. It became a prosperous center of commerce, particularly with traders from India, and remained powerful until the eleventh century CE.

The Pagan Kingdom

Farther north, a group of people called the Burmans established a settlement called Pagan during the ninth century CE. The city grew in power and influence and became the center of the Pagan kingdom. In 1044, a man named Anawrahta came to power. In the years ahead, he forged a series of reforms that would create the basis for the nation that exists today. For example, he created alliances with neighboring groups. He established an irrigation system so more crops could be grown. Anawrahta promoted Theravada Buddhism and ensured that it was taught throughout his empire. He widened Burmese influence by expanding trade and shipping routes, which in turn spread the use of the Burmese language.

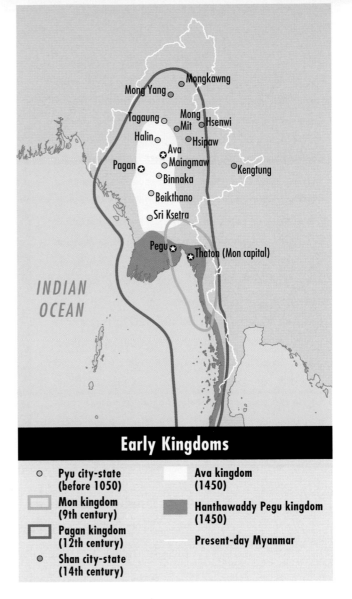

Early Kingdoms

○ Pyu city-state (before 1050)	☐ Ava kingdom (1450)
☐ Mon kingdom (9th century)	■ Hanthawaddy Pegu kingdom (1450)
☐ Pagan kingdom (12th century)	— Present-day Myanmar
● Shan city-state (14th century)	

Pagan

The ancient city of Pagan is one of the oldest settlements in Myanmar. Located in the Mandalay region, it lies near the geographical center of the nation. No one is exactly sure how old Pagan is. It may have been founded in the second century BCE, but more likely it was founded in the 800s CE. It became the capital of the Pagan kingdom and the cultural heart of Burma, attracting some of the day's greatest thinkers in religion, philosophy, languages, medicine, and law. Religion was the focus of the city for centuries, and eventually more than ten thousand Buddhist structures were built there. The city never recovered after Mongol armies attacked the kingdom in the late 1200s. Pagan is in a region frequently shaken by earthquakes. These quakes have destroyed many of the site's temples and pagodas, but more than two thousand remain. Today, Pagan is a popular tourist destination, as people come to experience the eerie landscape filled with temples.

Decline of Pagan

The Pagan kingdom was beginning to lose influence in the Irrawaddy Valley by the mid-thirteenth century. The Pagan leaders began to feel pressure from a people known as the Shan, who had established settlements along the edge of the Pagan kingdom. They came under greater threat from another group known as the Mongols. Originating in central Asia, the Mongols eventually controlled the largest land empire in history, stretching from the eastern edge of China all the way to Europe. The Mongols invaded Pagan in 1277. The two groups fought for years, leading to the end of Pagan rule.

In the centuries that followed, the Irrawaddy Valley region lost its political unity and existed more as a collection of small semi-independent kingdoms. These included the Ava, the Hanthawaddy Pegu, and the Shan. Like the Pagan leaders, the Ava kings encouraged education and literature. The Ava considered themselves the successors of the Pagan kingdom, but they failed to establish the same broad influence. The Hanthawaddy Pegu were a rival of the Ava, and many

King Razadarit ruled the Hanthawaddy Pegu kingdom in the late 1300s and early 1400s. He unified the people of southern Burma, and together they fought the Ava kingdom of the north.

historians consider them the most successful of these mini-kingdoms, enjoying a period of robust prosperity during the 1400s and early 1500s. The Shan entrenched themselves in the northeastern areas of Burma and remained in power for about three centuries, before declining in the mid-1500s.

Toungoo and Konbaung Dynasties

■ Toungoo dynasty, 1485–1752

□ Konbaung dynasty, 1857–1885

— Present-day Myanmar

Toungoo to Konbaung

As Ava was becoming unstable in the early 1500s, a small section of the kingdom known as Toungoo declared itself independent. As the century progressed, Toungoo's influence and power grew under the guidance of its king, Tabinshwehti. By mid-century, Toungoo had claimed most of the territory once under the control of Pagan. Under Bayinnaung, the leader after Tabinshwehti, the expansion continued. As the 1500s came to a close, Toungoo was in control of vast stretches of Southeast Asia. This included the Shan regions, Siam (now Thailand), and Manipur (now part of India). The Toungoo rule remained in place in various forms, even through periods of rebellion, warfare, and economic instability, until the mid-1700s.

By the end of the 1750s, a new

dynasty, the Konbaung, was expanding its area of control in Burma. The Konbaung dynasty was led by King Alaungpaya, who created a largely unified Burma, mostly though sheer military force. He wiped out most remnants of the mini-kingdoms. He also weakened the outside influences, including the French and the English, who were meddling in Burma and dividing the nation. This military approach to governing would lead to an almost constant state of conflict for generations. For example, over the next hundred years, Burma was at war with nearby Siam almost constantly, and for a time it battled with China as well. Burma also moved into the region called Assam, to the northwest, now part of India. This brought Burma into conflict with the powerful British Empire, which controlled most of India.

Military practice during the Konbaung dynasty. The Konbaung dynasty battled neighboring kingdoms and eventually became one of the largest Burmese dynasties.

A Long History **45**

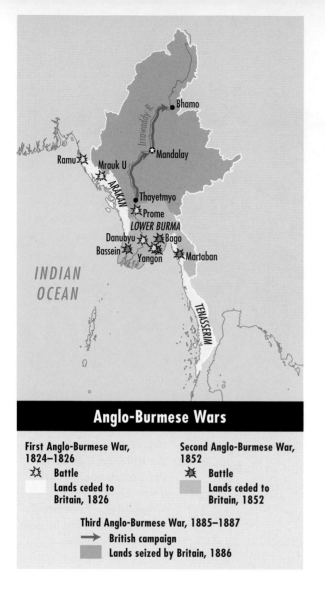

In 1824, this conflict became the First Anglo-Burmese War, in which the Burmese fought the more numerous and better-funded British forces. The result was a devastating loss for Burma in terms of military force, money, land, and regional influence. The Burmese and the British battled more times in the years ahead. The Second Anglo-Burmese War took place in 1852, and the Third Anglo-Burmese War spanned 1885 to 1887. This war resulted in the exile of the final Burmese king, Thibaw. The British were now in charge of Burma.

Into the Twentieth Century

Great Britain made swift and radical changes to Burmese society. The importance of religion—Buddhism in particular—was diminished. Burma became classified as a province of India. The British cleared the Irrawaddy Delta of mangrove trees and other plants and planted the land with rice, which had become a valuable export product. In the mid-nineteenth century, only about 60,000 acres (24,000 hectares) of land in Lower Burma was used to grow rice. By the 1940s, rice was being grown on 10,000,000 acres (4,000,000 ha) in the region. Many Burmese moved from northern regions to Lower Burma to work in the rice industry.

While British influence did lead to greater economic prosperity, it was rarely shared among the Burmese people. Instead, it went to British leaders and a few favored Indians. There were some revolts against the British oppression, but they were usually dealt with in a brutal fashion. In 1930, for example, a Buddhist monk named Saya San led an uprising of poor farmers. Saya San's rebels were armed only with swords and spears. The British guns soon overwhelmed them. More than ten thousand Burmese were killed in the uprising, and Saya San was captured and hanged.

Burmese farmers plow a rice paddy in the early twentieth century.

Toward Independence

As the twentieth century progressed, the relationship between the Burmese and the British calmed. Many young Burmese people were ready to embrace a carefully planned push for Burmese independence. Soon, a younger and more determined generation was protesting. Students and other intellectuals were hoping to reclaim their heritage and place in society. In 1936, university students went on strike under the leadership of Aung San, who would become known as the father of Burma, and Thakin Nu, who would later be known as U Nu and become the nation's first prime minister. This

Ne Win (left) and Aung San (right) were part of the student anticolonial movement known as Thakin. Ne Win would eventually become prime minister and head of state, while Aung San would become the leading force in the independence movement.

anticolonial movement was known as Thakin, the Burmese word for "master." The Burmese were required to use the term when addressing a British person, so the students reclaimed the word to show that they were in fact the masters of their own land.

Soon, the strikes were reaching beyond temples and universities to streets and businesses of ordinary neighborhoods. In 1937, the British responded to the protests by separating Burma from Indian rule. The British also gave Burma its own constitution. But the fact that Burma was still under British rule did not sit well with the Burmese people.

When World War II broke out in 1939, Burmese leaders such as Aung San saw it as an opportunity. The Burmese should only help the British with the war effort, they argued, if Great Britain granted Burma more concessions. By 1941, the British were also fighting Japan, and some Burmese thought it

U Thant Museum

In 2013, work began on construction of a museum in honor of Burmese native U Thant. Born in 1909 into a wealthy family of landowners, U Thant grew up during a particularly tense period of British rule in Burma. He was an avid reader as a boy and wanted to be a journalist in adulthood. But during his years in college he became friends with the man later known as U Nu, who would serve as Burma's prime minister following the nation's independence from Great Britain after World War II. Through U Nu, U Thant gained significant political power. He soon gained a reputation for levelheadedness in times of crisis. In 1961, he was appointed secretary general of the United Nations, an international organization dedicated to solving conflicts between nations around the world. U Thant served in that position until the end of 1971. He died in 1974, having distinguished himself as one of the most noted Burmese citizens in history. The museum that now stands in his honor in Yangon is called the U Thant House and is dedicated to his life, work, and philosophies.

would be better to side with Japan in exchange for promises of full independence after the war's conclusion. Japan eventually occupied much of Burma during the war, and Burmese forces aided them in battle. As a result, nearly a quarter of a million Burmese lost their lives in the war.

After World War II, the British still controlled Burma, but they agreed that the nation should become independent. In 1947, the Panglong Agreement determined the borders that define Myanmar to this day. On January 4, 1948, the nation formally became independent.

Army vehicles guard government buildings after the military seized power in 1962.

The Young Nation

In Myanmar's early years of independence, it functioned under a democratic system in which leaders were elected. But the young nation was unstable, and the central government and the military had a difficult time trying to keep the nation unified.

The democracy was still in its infancy when a military coup occurred in March 1962. The coup, or overthrow of the government, was led by Ne Win, a former commander of Myanmar's armed forces as well as the nation's acting prime minister in the late 1950s. Ne Win and his followers declared Myanmar's young democracy unsuitable and vowed to establish a more socialist order. Military forces then seized control of most of Myanmar's businesses. The government, barely able to run itself, would run all major industries as well.

The economic results were disastrous. Myanmar became one of the poorest countries in the world.

Ne Win also launched an era of isolationism from the rest of the world. He and his advisers wanted Myanmar to have as little interaction as possible with the international community.

Troubled Times

In time, politicians were replaced by military leaders, and the military leaders became the ruling class. By the late 1980s, the economy had improved in some respects. Military leaders loosened restrictions on some business pursuits among private individuals. The government maintained control of the major

Ne Win (center) remained in power for twenty-six years after the 1962 coup.

People fill the streets of Yangon during a pro-democracy rally in 1988.

industries, but it allowed certain smaller businesses to grow and encouraged investment from other countries.

The government of Myanmar administered its policies through bullying, intimidation, and violence. The Burmese people showed their dissatisfaction with the nation's leadership in various ways. There were rebellions, student demonstrations, and street protests that were swiftly put down.

One of the most horrific examples of this came with the so-called 8888 Uprising, which got its name because it began on August 8, 1988 (8/8/88). The uprising started as a bold student protest against the government's economic missteps. It grew rapidly into a statement against the government's refusal to provide a more open and democratic society, and against the repression of basic human rights, including religious freedom. The protest soon involved hundreds of thousands of citizens,

Burmese soldiers force demonstrators from the streets during the summer of 1988.

including dozens of Buddhist monks. The protests grew so large that some people thought Myanmar was going to have a revolution. In the face of this, military forces under General Saw Maung seized control of the government. Saw Maung immediately moved to end the demonstrations. Thousands of protesters were killed.

People around the world responded with disgust to the Burmese government's human rights abuses. Yet the Burmese leadership made no concessions. In the late twentieth century, other nations began applying pressure on Myanmar through sanctions. For example, Western businesses were given incentives to cut all ties with Myanmar, denying it an array of critical goods and services. People also refused to buy products from Myanmar, denying the military government millions of dollars in revenues.

Making Progress

A growing internal movement toward democracy began gaining strength in spite of repeated crackdowns, and by 2008 a new constitution with a nod toward genuine democratic reforms was being developed. Meanwhile, new laws were forged to make many of the old government's repressive practices illegal.

In 2010, elections including political parties outside military control were held. As a result, the military's power in Myanmar was reduced to some degree. Unfortunately, there

Demonstrators in the Philippines condemn the 2010 elections in Myanmar as unfair. The ruthless actions of Myanmar's leadership frequently aroused protests around the world.

appeared to be widespread fraud committed by military factions in order to retain as much influence as possible.

Another round of elections in 2012 appeared to have been more fair. The National League for Democracy (NLD), a party with no military ties, did very well.

Then, in 2015, elections were again held, and the NLD swept into power. The NLD won a large majority of the elected seats in the national legislature. The military, however, retains considerable power in the government.

Supporters of the NLD cheer as they wait for voting results on election night in 2015.

Myanmar has also made economic reforms in recent years. Its closest neighbors, notably China, Singapore, Thailand, and India, have begun loaning the nation the funds it needs to expand its economy. The United States has relaxed many sanctions that denied Myanmar trade opportunities. In addition, some nations that had loaned Myanmar money in the past, including France, Norway, and Japan, are helping Myanmar. These nations have agreed either that Myanmar does not have to pay back all of the loans, or that it can pay the money back over more time than originally planned.

In recent years, Myanmar has been moving forward both politically and economically. As it does, the world watches carefully, hoping that the young nation will continue to make progress.

Small boats pass huge ships at the busy port of Yangon.

CHAPTER 5

Governing Myanmar

SINCE GAINING ITS POLITICAL INDEPENDENCE IN 1948, Myanmar has struggled to establish a democracy. From 1962 through 2011, it was ruled by a series of military juntas (councils). During this time, the nation was largely isolated from the rest of the world. The juntas suppressed political opponents while committing human rights atrocities against some people. In recent years, however, fair elections have been held, and Myanmar appears to be making strides toward becoming a democratic nation.

Opposite: **A flag is raised during a ceremony in the capital city of Nay Pyi Taw.**

Regional Government

Just as the United States is divided into states, Myanmar is divided into smaller sections that are governed individually as well as overseen by the national government. In Myanmar's case, these smaller units are called regions and states. Myanmar has fourteen in total—seven regions and seven states. Regions are areas of Myanmar populated predominantly by the Bamar

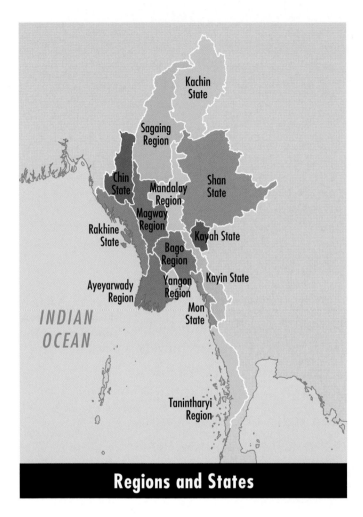

Regions and States

ethnic group, the most common one in Myanmar. States are populated by a minority ethnic group. There are also a small number of self-governed partitions populated by even smaller ethnic groups. Within the regions and states are smaller sections called districts, townships, towns, cities, wards, and villages.

Political Parties

Myanmar has many political parties—but just two of them hold the bulk of the political influence. The Union Solidarity and Development Party (USDP), which was founded in 2010, is the more conservative of the two major parties and carries echoes of the nation's former military rule. The other major party is the more liberal National League for Democracy (NLD), which was founded in 1988 and won a landslide election in 2015 that gave it control of the government. The leader of the NLD is Aung San Suu Kyi, who won the Nobel Peace Prize in 1991 for her pro-democracy efforts.

A Life of Courage

One of the most notable political figures in Myanmar's long history is Aung San Suu Kyi (1945–). Her father, Aung San, was a man of great political fame. He helped found the Burmese army and negotiated for Myanmar's independence from Great Britain in the aftermath of World War II. Her mother was no less notable in political circles, serving as an ambassador to both India and Nepal.

Aung San Suu Kyi attended college abroad, receiving a degree from Oxford University in England in philosophy, politics, and economics in 1969. In the 1970s, she worked at the United Nations, and in the 1980s she returned to Myanmar to care for her sick mother.

During this decade, she also became active in the pro-democracy movement that opposed the oppressive military regime. She was placed under house arrest (not allowed to leave her own house) in 1989. All this did was

increase her popularity among Burmese people, and her political party, the National League for Democracy, did very well in the 1990 election. But the military government refused to acknowledge the party's victory and blocked Aung San Suu Kyi from taking power.

She received the Nobel Peace Prize in 1991 for her pro-democracy work. In subsequent years, the military leadership tried its best to quell her growing influence on the Burmese population, as well as her popularity around the world, but to little avail. She remained under house arrest on and off in the following years. She was again released from house arrest in November 2010 and has since built strong relationships with powerful political figures around the globe.

She was elected to the Burmese House of Representatives in 2012. In the 2015 election, the NLD won control of the government, and Aung San Suu Kyi became, in effect, the leader of the country. She has been an inspiration to millions as an icon of personal freedom and independent thought.

Other political parties with some small influence in the Burmese government include the National Unity Party, the Pa-O National Organization, the Wa National Unity Party, and the All Mon Region Democracy Party. Some military factions also retain the ability to appoint individuals to various political positions.

Executive Branch

Like the government of the United States, the government of Myanmar has three separate branches—executive, legislative,

Myanmar's National Government

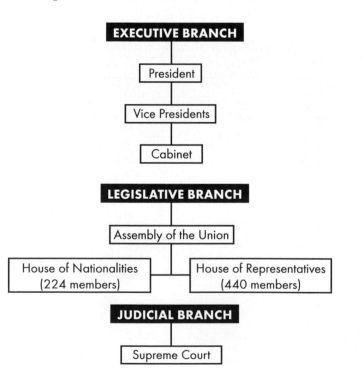

Thein Sein, the president of Myanmar from 2011 to 2016, was born in a small village near the Irrawaddy River in 1945. His family was poor, his father grinding out a living as a farmer and laborer. Thein Sein attended the Defense Services Academy and then joined the military. He had a distinguished military career for the next four decades, eventually attaining the rank of four-star general in 2004. Three years later, in 2007, he was made Myanmar's prime minister by the ruling military junta at the time. In 2010, he formally retired from the military and ran for a seat in the legislature as a candidate in the Union Solidarity and Development Party. He won and was then chosen to be president in March 2011.

As president, Thein Sein was noted for relaxing the government's heavy censorship of the media and for supervising the release of numerous political prisoners. In 2012, he met with Barack Obama, making him the first leader of Myanmar to meet with a U.S. president since the 1960s.

and judicial. Also like the United States, the head of the executive branch is called the president. But unlike in the United States, in Myanmar the president is chosen by the House of Representatives. The Burmese president is the head of the cabinet, which includes over two dozen ministers. Each minister oversees a different area, such as education, defense, health, and industry. The Burmese executive branch differs from the U.S. executive branch in that it has three different vice presidents.

The National Flag

The current flag of Myanmar is simple and distinctive. It features three horizontal stripes of equal size—yellow at the top, green in the middle, and red at the bottom—with a large white star overlaying all three in the center. This design was officially adopted in 2010. The large white star symbolizes the union of the country. The yellow bar represents solidarity among the people, the green stands for peace and tranquility, and the red symbolizes courage and decisiveness.

Legislative Branch

Myanmar's lawmaking body is called the Assembly of the Union. It is divided into two parts. The House of Representatives has 440 members, who represent different

Myanmar's House of Representatives in session

National Anthem

The national anthem of Myanmar is "Kaba Ma Kyei" ("Till the End of the World"). Saya Tin (right), a member of a group that was fighting for Burmese independence, wrote the lyrics in 1930. The British arrested him for inciting rebellion following the first performance of the song on July 20, 1930. He remained jailed until 1946. The song was adopted as the Burmese national anthem in 1947.

Burmese lyrics

Ga ba ma kyae, myan ma pyi,
Do bo bwa a mwae sit mo chit myat no bae.
Ga ba ma kyae, myan ma pyi,
Do bo bwa a mwae sit mo chit myat no bae.
Pyi daung zu go a thèt pae lo to ka kwè ma lae,
Da do byae da do myae do paing dae myae.
Do byae do myae a kyo go nyi nya zwa do da twae
Tan saung ba so lae do da(u) win bay a po tan myae.

English translation

'Til the end of the world, Myanmar!
Since she is the true inheritance from our forefathers,
we love and value her.
'Til the end of the world, Myanmar!
Since she is the true inheritance from our forefathers,
we love and value her.
We will fight and give our lives for the union
This is the country and land of our own
For her prosperity, we will responsibly shoulder the task,
Standing as one in duty to our precious land.

An activist is surrounded by a crowd at the court where he is being tried on charges related to his protest of a copper mine project. He was convicted at the trial and sentenced to hard labor as well as prison.

areas based upon population. The House of Nationalities has 224 members, sixteen from each state and region. About three-quarters of each house is elected, and one-quarter is appointed by the military. All legislators serve five-year terms.

Judicial Branch

The highest court in Myanmar is the Supreme Court. The nation also has many lower courts at the state, district, and town levels. Myanmar's courts have come under heavy criticism from the international community over the years. The court system is heavily influenced by the military and has often failed to provide fair trials or reasonable punishments. Many people have been imprisoned unjustly for long periods, and some have been tortured.

Armed Forces

The Burmese military includes an army, navy, and air force, as well as the police force and local militia. The army is the largest part of the military, with more than three hundred thousand soldiers. The army is primarily used to combat rebels within the country. The Burmese navy is much smaller, with only about twenty thousand troops. It has a fleet of more

Members of Myanmar's military march in a parade on Armed Forces Day.

than 125 ships. As Myanmar's involvement with the rest of the world has grown, the nation's government has become increasingly protective of its waters.

The Burmese air force has also undergone notable upgrades in recent years, purchasing new crafts, weapons, and guidance systems. Nevertheless, this branch of Myanmar's military remains the weakest of the three, used mostly for domestic conflicts and crisis situations.

The Myanmar navy consists of many kinds of ships, including barges to transport supplies.

Meet the New Capital City

In 2006 Myanmar officially got a new capital city. Nay Pyi Taw, located in the south-central area of the nation, replaced Yangon as the nation's capital. Nay Pyi Taw is about as new a city as one can imagine, having been founded on open scrubland about 200 miles (320 km) north of Yangon in 2002. The Burmese leadership has insisted that the new site is better than Yangon because it is more centrally located and it provides a powerful government presence near the states of Shan, Kayin, and Kayah, which have been unstable in recent years. Others, however, believe that the leaders moved the capital because they believed Yangon, located near

Myanmar's southern coast, was too vulnerable to possible military attacks.

The city was built on a grand scale. It has twenty-lane highways and large shopping malls. It has restaurants, hotels, four golf courses, and a zoo. According to some estimates, by 2015, the population of Nay Pyi Taw had grown to 925,000. But many people believe that far fewer people actually live there. The vast roads are often completely empty of cars, and the restaurants sit quiet. The people who live in Nay Pyi Taw are primarily government workers. To some people, the deserted city feels like a movie set.

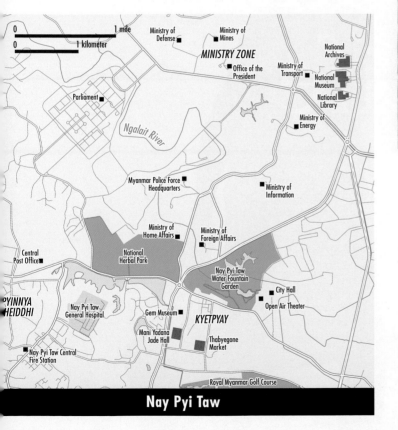

Nay Pyi Taw

CHAPTER 6

The Working Life

S INCE MYANMAR OPENED ITSELF UP TO FOREIGN investment in 1988, its economy has been growing. It has launched campaigns to improve its ability to do business, forged a series of laws designed to crack down on corruption, which has been rampant in Burmese business communities, and persuaded other nations to ease the sanctions that have been hampering its import and export opportunities.

Opposite: **A farmer sows rice seeds in a field in Myanmar. Many types of rice grow best in flooded fields.**

Agriculture

The most significant industry in Myanmar is agriculture. It accounts for more than a third of the nation's gross domestic product (GDP), the total value of all the goods and services produced in the country. The most important agricultural product is rice. About 60 percent of farmland is devoted to growing rice.

Other major crops include beans, peanuts, sugarcane, sesame, onions, and rubber. Much of the land is cleared in slash-and-burn fashion as global demand for Burmese products grows, and the bulk of the farmland lies in the nation's lower regions, where the water supply is greater and the soil is more fertile.

Common livestock in Myanmar includes pigs, cattle, goats, chickens, and water buffalo. Fishing is also important. Most of the fish are caught in the sea, but fish farms are also

Fishermen in Inle Lake wrap a leg around an oar to row, leaving their hands free to handle the nets.

becoming more common. Species such as tilapia and carp are raised on these farms.

Logging is an important business in Myanmar. Teak, in particular, is a popular wood. Myanmar is responsible for about 80 percent of the world's teak supply.

Mining

Another major source of Burmese revenue involves the mining of precious gems and stones. Burmese gemstones are considered among the world's best. Rubies from Myanmar, for example, are highly sought after and much prized. The Mogok region in the central part of the country produces about 90 percent of all the rubies in the world. Myanmar is also a plentiful source of jade, an ornamental stone that usually comes in a beautiful green color and can be carved into various forms. It is particularly popular in China.

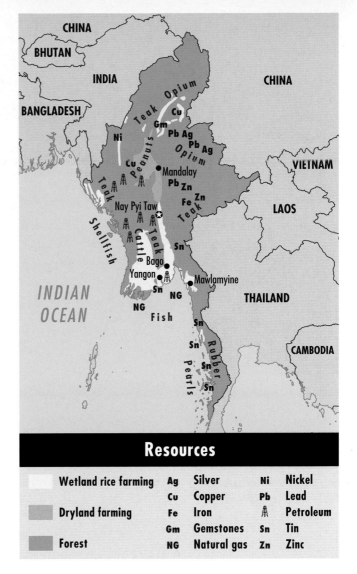

Myanmar also produces sapphires and pearls. The majority of Burmese gems are sold to neighboring Thailand.

While the quality of Myanmar's gems is rarely in doubt, mining methods used in the country have been criticized.

Young boys pan for rubies in the Mogok region of Myanmar.

Miners are often forced to work long hours in dangerous conditions, and they barely earn enough to survive. Sometimes these workers attempt to smuggle rough gems onto the black market for extra money, but that carries the risk of severe punishment. Treatment of these workers has been so harsh at times, in fact, that there have been international boycotts urging people to refuse purchase of Burmese jade and rubies.

Copper mining is a growing industry in Myanmar. Other minerals commonly dug out of the ground in the nation include lead, zinc, silver, and nickel. Myanmar is also a key exporter of charcoal. It produces around a million tons of charcoal each year.

Oil and Natural Gas

Myanmar is a steady supplier of oil and natural gas, particularly to its neighbors China and Thailand. In Myanmar, a company run by the government controls the oil and gas industry. It takes care of everything from exploring new sites to drilling, processing, and delivering the products. Foreign companies have invested millions of dollars to obtain the rights to explore offshore sites. Myanmar produces about 20,000 barrels of oil per day, and it is believed to have more than 50 million barrels still sitting in underground pools, waiting to be tapped. Myanmar also produces about 12 billion cubic meters of natural gas each year. The nation's natural gas reserves are believed to be about 300 billion cubic meters.

Money Facts

The basic unit of currency in Myanmar is the *kyat*. One hundred *pya* equals one kyat. The symbol for the kyat is a simple capital *K*. Burmese coins come in values of 1, 5, 10, 50, and 100 kyat. Bills have denominations of a half-kyat note worth 50 pyas, and 1, 5, 10, 20, 50, 100, 200, 500, 1,000, 5,000, and 10,000 kyat.

Most kyat bills feature the Chinthe—a lionlike creature often depicted in Myanmar—on the front. The 5,000-kyat note shows a white elephant, and the 10,000-kyat note bears the seal of Myanmar. The backs of Burmese banknotes feature typical Burmese scenes. For example, the 5-kyat note portrays a group of children playing a game called chinlone. In 2015, US$1.00 equaled about 1,280 kyat.

Manufacturing

Until the middle of the twentieth century, Myanmar had little manufacturing. Today, cigarette and cigar manufacturing is a major industry. The country also produces steel, textiles, machinery, transportation equipment, and cement. Smaller industries include paper production, food processing, and the manufacture of medicines.

Tourism

While many Asian countries enjoy considerable revenues through the tourism trade, Myanmar's tourism industry is just beginning to grow. It is undoubtedly a beautiful place with

What Myanmar Grows, Makes, and Mines

AGRICULTURE (2013)

Rice	28,000,000 metric tons
Sugarcane	9,900,000 metric tons
Beans	3,800,000 metric tons

MANUFACTURING

Textiles (2012)	US $846,000,000 in exports
Steel (2013)	30,000 metric tons
Cigarettes (2014)	462,000,000 packs

MINING

Copper (2010)	12,000 metric tons
Sapphires (2012)	1,351,916 carats
Rubies (2012)	852,033 carats

stunning scenery and a fascinating culture, but its reputation for military control, human rights violations, and political corruption have hampered efforts by the government to draw tourist dollars. About a million people visit Myanmar each year, just a fraction of those that travel to other Asian locales.

Drug Trade

Myanmar is one of the leading sources of illegal drugs in Southeast Asia. It is, for example, one of the world's largest producers of opium. Opium, a by-product of the poppy plant, is used to make the dangerous drug heroin. Many farmers in Myanmar grow poppies because the opium is much more profitable than other agricultural crops. Most of Myanmar's opium production occurs in the northeastern part of the country, where it generates hundreds of millions of dollars in revenue each year. Another common drug produced in Myanmar is

Tourists take pictures at a pagoda in the ancient city of Pagan. The number of foreign tourists visiting Myanmar has increased dramatically in recent years, rising from about 760,000 in 2009 to more than 2 million in 2013.

Farmers harvest poppies in northeastern Myanmar. Poppies are an important part of the economy in the region.

methamphetamine. Myanmar is, in fact, the world's single largest producer of methamphetamines. Many of the drugs produced in Myanmar are exported to China and Thailand, and from there to the rest of the world. In Myanmar, illegal drugs of one kind or another generate from US$1.5 to US$2 billion in revenue each year.

Investor Interest

Foreigners have had a growing interest in investing in Myanmar in recent years, although not nearly as much as the current Burmese government and business leaders would prefer. People from China, India, and Singapore have been the most willing to invest, but many in the world beyond have remained wary. Decades of sanctions by the United States, the United Kingdom, and other nations have made Myanmar an unattractive financial risk. And while many of these sanctions have been lifted in recent times, ongoing concerns about human rights violations, corrupt leadership, and influence by the Burmese military remain high. In addition, Myanmar's infrastructure—its roads, ports, and communications systems—needs to be upgraded. Many roads remain unpaved, and electricity shortages are fairly common. Furthermore, much of Myanmar's workforce is undereducated. Nevertheless, some business experts see tremendous potential in Myanmar, and with a more reform-minded government in place, the potential to move in a positive direction is at hand.

Many people in Myanmar use animals to work the land and haul goods.

At Work

There are about twenty million adults in Myanmar who work. Roughly two-thirds of them are employed in agriculture. There are two types of jobs—public sector and private sector. Public sector means working for the government. In most cases, public sector employees in Myanmar work five days a week for a total of about thirty-five hours. In the private sector, Burmese usually work a bit longer. Six-day workweeks, with a total of fifty hours or more, are not unusual. In many industries, opportunities for advancement are limited. People who work in cities tend to be paid better than people in rural areas.

Textile manufacturing is one of Myanmar's fastest-growing industries. As of 2014, two new textile factories were opening in the nation every week.

A child works in a cigar factory near Inle Lake. People working in these factories often roll five hundred cigars a day.

Average pay is about US$1,000 per year. The cost of living is much lower than it is in many other countries. Still, the average worker doesn't have much left over after covering necessities. Laws require employers to provide overtime pay, but these laws are often poorly enforced.

Working conditions for the average Burmese citizen have improved since the days of full military control, although there is still much room for improvement. Child labor also continues to be a problem. Legally, children are required to attend school through the elementary grades. But in areas of the country where there is little enforcement of such rules, children sometimes have no choice but to skip school and help support their family.

CHAPTER 7

People and Language

THE NATION OF MYANMAR IS HOME TO ABOUT 51.4 million people. The average Burmese person lives to be sixty-six years old. In the United States, by comparison, the life expectancy is seventy-nine years. On average, Burmese women have two children. Unlike in many countries, Burmese women are not pressured to settle down and have children.

Ethnic Groups

The people of Myanmar are very diverse. They speak many different languages and come from many different ethnic groups, each with their own customs.

The largest group in Myanmar is the Burmans. About two-thirds of all Burmese people are Burman. It is believed that the ancestors of the Burmans migrated from the Yunnan region of southwestern China about 1,500 years ago. They settled along

Population of Major Cities (2015 est.)	
Yangon	4,477,638
Mandalay	1,208,099
Nay Pyi Taw	925,000
Mawlamyine	438,861
Bago	244,376

| CHINA |
| BHUTAN |
| INDIA |
| BANGLADESH |

Mandalay

Nay Pyi Taw ☆

Bago
Yangon

Mawlamyine

INDIAN OCEAN

CHINA

VIETNAM

LAOS

THAILAND

CAMBODIA

Persons per square mile		Persons per square kilometer
more than 520		more than 200
261–520		101–200
131–260		51–100
27–130		11–50
3–26		1–10
fewer than 3		fewer than 1

Ethnic Population in Myanmar

Burman	68%
Shan	9%
Karen	7%
Rakhine	3.5%
Chinese	2.5%
Mon	2%
Kachin	1.5%
Indian	1.25%
Kayah	0.75%
Other	4.5%

the Irrawaddy River. Many older Burman people wear traditional clothes such as sarongs. A sarong is a length of fabric that is wrapped around the waist to cover the lower half of the body. Younger Burmans, on the other hand, are more likely to wear Western-style clothes such as jeans, T-shirts, and sneakers. Most Burmans follow the Theravada form of Buddhism. Thailand and Singapore are also home to large numbers of Burmans.

The second-largest ethnic group in Myanmar is the Shan. About five million Shan live in Myanmar. Most are in the Shan State, which makes up the nation's eastern quarter. Like the Burmans, most Shan are dedicated Theravada Buddhists. Many of them are farmers and artisans. Many Shan desire independence from Myanmar, and this has sometimes led to armed conflict between Shan rebels and the Burmese military. During

About fifty thousand people live in Mae La refugee camp in Thailand. The vast majority of them are Karen people from Myanmar.

Some women in the Paudang ethnic group, a subgroup of the Kayah people, stretch their necks. They begin wearing brass coils, which push down on the collar bone, when they are children and gradually add more coils.

these battles, members of the Shan forces have often been forced to seek shelter in nearby Thailand. Also, Shan people are often treated poorly by the Burman majority in Myanmar, so many Shan have fled to Thailand as refugees. They are often treated just as poorly there, however, having to work under bad conditions for little pay. Thus, many Shan look to the day when they can become an independent nation with a sympathetic and representative government.

Other, smaller ethnic groups in Myanmar include the Karen, Kayah, Mon, Kachin, and Chin. The Karen people live in the lowlands and in the Bago Mountains. They have often fought the majority Burman people, and have battled for more autonomy. The government has responded brutally to the rebel Karen, burning villages. Tens of thousands of Karen refugees have fled to Thailand.

The Kayah live in the southern part of the Shan Plateau. Traditionally, they often wore red clothes, so they have sometimes been called the Red Karen. Like the Karen, they have often been in conflict with the Burmese government.

The Mon people live in eastern Myanmar. To a greater extent than with many other groups, the Mon people have

More than one million ethnic Kachin people live in Myanmar, most in Kachin State.

The Burmese alphabet includes thirty-three rounded letters.

merged with the Burman majority. Though many call themselves Mon, most now speak the Burmese language.

The Kachin people live in the northern part of Myanmar, near China. Their ancestors probably migrated there from central Asia. The Kachin people are made up of many different small groups speaking many different languages. Like many ethnic minorities in Myanmar, the Kachin have often faced discrimination by the government.

The Chin, who are descended from Mongol peoples of central Asia, live in the western hills near India. They live in large villages and grow rice, millet, and other crops.

There are also significant numbers of Chinese, Thai, and Indian people living in Myanmar.

Language

The people of Myanmar speak about ninety different languages. Some of the languages are so ancient that they are kept alive only by tiny communities living in remote locations. Even in those instances, there may be just a handful of people who are truly fluent.

The most common language spoken in the country is Burmese. It is the first language of more than thirty million residents of the country and the second language of another ten million. It is recognized in Myanmar's constitution as the nation's official language. The most common dialect, or version, of Burmese originated in the Irrawaddy River valley and is known as the Mandalay-Yangon dialect. Other dialects, which are found in areas beyond the Irrawaddy, include Merguese, Intha, and Arakanese. Although these dialects differ greatly, people who speak different dialects can still communicate with one another.

Common Burmese Phrases

Min-ga-la-ba	Hello
Kamya ne-kaun-la?	How are you?
Kamya ne-meh beh-lo k'aw-leh?	What's your name?
Sain bhaalkalell?	Where are you from?
Kan-kaung-ba-zay	Good luck
Shin aaingaliutlo pyaw lar?	Do you speak English?
Ce-zu tin-bah-deh	Thank you
Bhine	Good-bye

The second most common language in Myanmar is Shan, spoken mostly by the Shan people of the Shan State. Roughly three million people in Myanmar speak it. There are three main dialects, divided into three geographical areas of the Shan State—north, south, and east. The northern version, known as Lashio, is tinged with influences from nearby China. The southern variant, Taunggyi, is spoken mostly in the Shan capital. And the eastern dialect, called Kengtung, is found mostly

Many Shan people speak the Shan language, which is related to Thai.

in an area known as the Golden Triangle—a mountainous area where the borders of Myanmar, Laos, and Thailand meet.

Other languages commonly spoken in Myanmar include Karen, Kachin, Chin, and Mon. In addition, English is taught in some Burmese schools, but mostly among the upper classes. It is therefore used mostly by upper-class Burmese and is rarely spoken outside urban areas.

A man sells newspapers on the street in Yangon. Until 2012, the government limited what was printed in newspapers. Today, the press has greater freedom.

CHAPTER 8

The Spiritual World

MYTH AND RELIGION HAVE LONG BEEN CENTRAL to the lives of the Burmese people. Many of the traditions observed today have been passed on through generations for centuries. People in Myanmar who consider themselves deeply religious—which is a large proportion of the population—do not look upon religion as a single facet of their life the way many people do in the West. Instead, they see religion as a guiding force that informs everything they do.

Buddhism

Although Myanmar does not have an official religion, Theravada Buddhism is by far the most widely practiced religion in the country. Theravada Buddhism involves the rejection of worldly attachments as part of the greater quest for nirvana, freedom from the cycle of pain caused by the desire for worldly goods. Theravada is one of the most celebrated branches of Buddhism,

Major Religions in Myanmar

Buddhism	89%
Christianity	4%
Islam	4%
Other (Hindusim, folk religions, etc.)	3%

Buddhist nuns pray at Shwedagon Pagoda. Buddhist nuns and monks shave their heads to help eliminate their egos.

based on the oldest Buddhist teachings in the world. It is popular throughout Southeast Asia, practiced by significant majorities in Cambodia, Thailand, Sri Lanka, and Laos.

The earliest traces of Theravada are from about the fourth century BCE. By about the tenth century CE, it was flourishing in Burma. In the early twentieth century, a monk named U Narada revived a meditation approach called Vipassana, which had faded in usage over the years. Narada's variation of Theravada became so widely accepted that it is now often called the New Burmese Method.

Theravada monks are active members of Burmese society and are held in high regard. They are easily recognized in their long, simple robes and leather sandals. The color of a Buddhist

In Myanmar, Buddhist monks and nuns collect donations of food every day. They then use this food to help feed people in need.

monk's robes can differ from country to country. In Myanmar, they are most commonly a reddish brown, whereas in many other parts of Southeast Asia they are yellow.

Shwedagon Pagoda

Located in the former capital city of Yangon, the Shwedagon Pagoda is one of the most important landmarks in the nation. It is a gold-covered stupa—a towering, round structure containing Buddhist artifacts. Shwedagon Pagoda was built by the Mon people more than a thousand years ago. It has a soaring conical shape, with a point that reaches about 325 feet (99 m) into the sky. There are more than seven thousand diamonds and rubies at the top, with the very tip occupied by a stunning 76-carat diamond. The building's outside is covered in gold plating. Shwedagon Pagoda has four entrances, each guarded by a pair of imposing statues of lionlike creatures called leogryphs. Today, tourists are welcome to visit the pagoda, although some areas are off-limits to everyone but Buddhist monks.

The Spiritual World **95**

Other Religions

Other religions are also observed in Myanmar. One of the most common religions is Christianity. About 3 percent of the population belongs to Protestant groups, and another 1 percent is Roman Catholic. Many ethnic minorities in Myanmar are Christian. About 80 percent of the Chin people are Christian. The Kachin are primarily Baptist and Roman Catholic. Many Karen and Kaya are also Christian.

A priest leads a Christian service in the hills of Myanmar.

Islam is another common religion, followed by about 4 percent of the people. Muslims live in all parts of Myanmar. Other Burmese people subscribe to Hinduism, the most practiced religion in neighboring India. Thus, the great majority of Burmese citizens who follow it are of Indian descent.

Government Persecution

The government has sometimes restricted followers of Christianity, Hinduism, Islam, and other religions, often refusing them the opportunity to maintain their houses of worship or the right to build new ones. Muslims have been attacked violently on many occasions.

The Rohingya people, Muslims who live in Rakhine State in western Myanmar, have been treated particularly harshly.

A Bangladeshi official comforts an exhausted Rohingya Muslim family that has fled violence in Myanmar.

The government claims they are not Burmese citizens even though some Rohingya people have lived there for many generations. The government has also limited Rohingya people to having just two children. Many Rohingyas have been forced from their homes because of violence, and tens of thousands have fled the country in boats. Most have ended up in Bangladesh and Malaysia.

Non-Buddhists have a difficult time gaining ground in Burmese society, especially in the government or military. Young people are often pressured to become Buddhists, and anyone looking to move up in military rank has little hope of doing so while subscribing to any other faith.

Folklore and Mythology

Myanmar has a rich and varied folklore and mythology. These ancient stories are populated with fantastic creatures of all types, which have powers and personality traits that make them seem more human than fantastical. Many of the stories arose centuries ago and were passed down from one generation to the next. Many pass along important philosophical lessons to the audience.

In Myanmar, puppets are sometimes used to tell folktales.

Perhaps the most popular creatures in Burmese folklore are the belu. There are two kinds of belu, one evil and one good-hearted. The evil belu is an ogre or a demon, depending on the story. It has long fangs, is quick to anger, and has the habit of eating people. The average belu looks human most of the time, but it has the ability to change its shape, making it all the more dangerous. The good-hearted form of the belu is the complete opposite, taking up righteous causes and eating only plant parts like flowers and berries.

A carving of a smiling belu at Shwedagon Pagoda

Another important creature from Burmese folklore is the asura. It comes from Buddhism and represents the lowest of gods. Even though they are ranked above humans, asuras are riddled with bad traits such as a quest for power, a hunger for pleasure, and a sense of superiority over all others. Asuras also have forceful personalities and are willing to fight to get what they want. According to legend, the asuras once occupied the highest levels of Mount Sumeru, the central mountain in the Buddhist world, along with all the other gods. Then they drank too much celebrating the arrival of a new ruler, Sakra. Disgusted by their behavior, Sakra banished them to the lowest levels of Mount Sumeru, where their anger and humiliation made them increasingly hostile.

A depiction of an asura in a temple. Asuras are said to possess bad traits such as envy, pride, and anger.

The hintha is a mythological aquatic bird that has represented many things in Burmese culture over the centuries. Most of them are positive, uplifting, and inspirational. The hintha is an important symbol used throughout Southeast Asia and India. It has signified everything from balance and harmony in one's life to purity, enlightenment, and great spiritual achievement. The hintha is celebrated for its ability to walk on land, fly in the air, and swim in the water, which together symbolize its great strength and personal freedom.

A large statue of a hintha is carried on a boat in a procession on Inle Lake.

A Tale From Shan

The Shan town of Pindaya is renowned for its limestone caves. They contain literally thousands of Buddhist images, including statues and inscriptions dating back hundreds of years, making the caves an important religious site. But the Pindaya caves are also known for something else—a giant spider.

According to legend, a giant spider once lived in the caves. One day, the spider came out of the cave and captured a local princess, dragging her in screaming terror back to its lair. When a prince heard of this, he went to the cave and slew the spider with a bow and arrow, winning the princess's heart. Upon killing the beast, the prince exclaimed "*Pinguya!*" which translates roughly as, "I have taken (killed) the spider!" Over time, the word *pinguya* transformed into *Pindaya*, which is how the town got its name.

CHAPTER 9

Arts and Sports

BURMESE LITERATURE DATES BACK HUNDREDS OF years. The earliest known examples are stone engravings. There are also old Burmese writings on dried palm leaves. Common writings included religious themes and poetry. Poems were crafted by people from all walks of life. Subjects of early Burmese poetry ranged from religious tales to epic histories to children's lullabies. In the 1700s, during the Konbaung dynasty, literature flourished, and some writers turned their talents to crafting plays. They found plays an excellent format for exploring ideas about society.

Opposite: **The "world's largest book" is located at Kuthodaw Pagoda in Mandalay. Its 1,460 pages were carved into stone between 1860 and 1868.**

The Written Word

Burma received its first printing press in 1816, a gift from a British missionary group that was dedicated to both free speech and spreading Christianity. With this new technology, Burmese writers were able to reach a much wider audience, which inspired new writers to come forward. People wrote Burmese histories, war chronicles, and commentary on social, political, and economic changes as they occurred around the nation. When the British took power in the 1820s, they brought along their own literary influences, forcing many Burmese people to embrace the English language. While this may have introduced new literary worlds, it also had another effect. By the start of the twentieth century, many Burmese had become so resentful of the British influence on their literature that they took actions to reestablish their own heritage. New forms of writing, from short stories and long novels to innovative poetic techniques, surfaced during this time,

British workers read while relaxing during the hot afternoon in Burma in 1910.

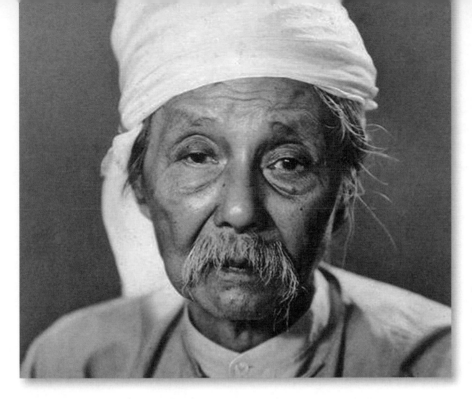

Thakin Kodaw Hmaing, considered one of Myanmar's greatest writers, was a member of the Thakin anticolonial movement in the 1930s.

incorporating nationalistic themes and Burmese traditions and folktales. Beginning in the 1910s, for example, poet and political leader Thakin Kodaw Hmaing wrote patriotic poems mocking Burmese politicians for fighting among themselves rather than against British colonialism. Many of these new writers were eager to point out the many hardships being suffered under colonial rule.

Following Burma's independence from Britain after World War II, the nation's new government claimed to support free thought. The government was supposedly completely supportive of Burmese writers. In truth, Burma's first independent government was more interested in supporting writers who supported the government. Then, in the 1960s, the government began aggressively censoring literature, choking off most forms of free expression and creativity. Burmese citizens were

Books are piled high at a used bookstore in Yangon.

still able to read and enjoy a variety of material, but much of it came from books written by people from other countries. Popular genre novels such as thrillers, Westerns, and romances could be found in Myanmar, but there were almost no books written by Burmese authors. Fiction writing was discouraged, because political leaders felt it had little value.

Today, with the military influence waning, censorship has loosened considerably. Burmese writers are becoming more common. Writers are addressing political themes and human rights issues, as well as depicting a sense of hopefulness for Myanmar's future. Some of the nation's most distinguished writers are also beginning to find support for their work at major publishing houses around the world.

Music

Myanmar has a variety of musical traditions. The classical forms of Burmese music have much in common with the music of nearby nations such as China. Some of the instruments commonly used in the performance of classical Burmese pieces include drums, bells, gongs, cymbals, pipes, flutes, xylophones, and stringed instruments like harps and zithers. Many classical Burmese songs were written hundreds of years ago. Common themes include royal celebrations, worship of mythical figures, and songs of sorrow.

The *saung gauk*, or Burmese harp, is considered the national instrument of Myanmar. A musician plays it sitting on the floor with the harp in his or her lap.

The dances that accompany classical Burmese music show the influence of neighboring nations. For example, many classical Burmese dances were adapted from those performed in Thailand. Both Burmese and Thai dance show the influence of Indian dance styles, with elaborate costumes and elegant and precise movements.

Myanmar also has a growing interest in modern music. It has been percolating underground for some time, in spite of the best efforts of the often repressive government. Western rock music began seeping into Burmese society as far back

A woman performs a classical Burmese dance. Many Burmese dances emphasize poses rather than motion.

A punk band performs at a festival in Yangon.

as the 1960s. It gained popularity quickly, but government leaders kept it from spreading through aggressive censorship campaigns. In the 1970s, the government screened all music being played on public radio, and by the 1980s music being produced by Burmese groups was being monitored carefully.

Still, young people found ways to hear, enjoy, and even produce the type of music they desired most, and in the 1990s rap and hip-hop became enormously popular. A Shan singer named Sai Sai Kham Leng is one of Myanmar's most popular rappers. More recently, heavy metal and punk have found a foothold among Burmese youth.

In 2012, the government outlawed all forms of musical censorship. With the loosening of restrictions on music, new groups have been surfacing at an astonishing rate. And with the power of the Internet, many of these groups can be heard across the world.

Min Wae Aung is one of Myanmar's best-known artists. His bright images of Buddhist monks hang in museums around the world.

The Visual Arts

The world of Burmese visual art is in a transition period. Since the nation earned its independence in 1948, the visual arts have been influenced by whatever government was in power at the time. During the socialist days, government leaders wanted artists to create works that supported their political beliefs. Artists could create what they wanted, but visual arts that fit what the government wanted received the most support. When the military took over, artists operated within more limited boundaries. Because of censorship, artists were limited to safe subjects such as landscapes, religious figures or tales, creatures from folklore, and famed military figures. If an artist tried to create material that was seen as threatening to the government, he or she would likely be punished. For example, in 1976 the painter Maung Theid Dhi received ten days in prison after displaying a self-portrait with one simple twist—the canvas had a chain around it to symbolize governmental oppression. Similarly, a painter named Bagyi Lynn Wunna used a peacock in some of his artwork in the 1990s. The peacock had long been a symbol of the royal family, and among Burmese students, it became a symbol representing dissatisfaction with the government. As a result, Wunna was sent to prison for a year.

Today's art scene in Myanmar is very different. The government abolished its censorship program in 2012. Since then, there has been an explosion of visual arts in Myanmar. There are more galleries, frequent public exhibits, and a ready availability of art supplies (restricting art supplies was one

With the changes in the government of Myanmar, artists such as Win Pe (left) now have great freedom to paint what they want.

In 2014, a gallery in Yangon held an exhibition featuring nothing but portraits of pro-democracy leader Aung San Suu Kyi.

way the government had discouraged creativity in earlier years). Many young talents are ready for their work to be seen. Artists now engage in depicting the political subjects that were once forbidden. They have created bold representations of contemporary hero and Nobel laureate Aung San Suu Kyi and her father, Aung San, who played a pivotal role in gaining Burma's independence from the British Empire and was eventually assassinated by his political enemies.

Many pieces of art that were created during the time of military oppression but were kept hidden are now being shown. This material provides a powerful glimpse into the fear that existed among the Burmese people. But these works are also a sign of hope and a reminder of how far the country has come, because artists can now express themselves openly for the first time.

A traditional sport in Myanmar is called chinlone. The game features groups of six players. The players pass around a small ball made of rattan, using only their feet, knees, and head. One of the players goes into the middle of the playing area and integrates the ball into a kind of dance, often passing it back to his fellow players, who have to then give it back to him with just a single kick. When the ball falls to the ground, the round is over. Chinlone is not a competitive sport in the sense that one player or team tries to outdo the other. Instead, it is judged based on how elegantly the game is played. Chinlone is popular in Myanmar and is played by both men and women, and by people of all ages. Adults and children often play together, and grandparents can enjoy playing the game with young children. Chinlone is commonly played in streets, yards, fields, and other open areas.

Sports

The most popular sport in Myanmar by far is soccer, which is called football throughout much of the world. Myanmar has a national team under the direction of the Myanmar Football Federation (MFF). The MFF has been in operation since 1947 and today administers all men's and women's teams as well as youth leagues and professional competitions.

Martial arts are also popular in Myanmar. Kickboxing tournaments are held in many parts of the country. Burmese martial arts include *banshay*, in which competitors use swords or long sticks called staffs, and *bando*, a fighting sport that uses no weapons.

CHAPTER 10

Everyday Life

LIFE IN MYANMAR ISN'T EASY FOR THE AVERAGE citizen. The Burmese people do not share many of the same luxuries that many people around the world take for granted every day. For many, simply surviving is a struggle. Still, with their natural sense of optimism about the future as well as the comfort they derive from their religious faith, the Burmese people persevere. And there is some evidence that better days are ahead for the nation as a whole.

Family and Community

Children learn from a very young age to respect their elders, and parents and grandparents play a significant role in making critical decisions for their children, much more so than in many Western families. In fact, Burmese children are less

Opposite: **A grandmother and child relax in their home.**

likely to go through a rebellious phase where they openly defy and challenge their parents. This may also be attributed to an unwritten rule in Burmese society that it is better to approach problems calmly and quietly than aggressively.

The Burmese are also known for being hardworking and efficient, making as much as possible out of what little they have. They are appreciative of all things and avoid being wasteful. Similarly, they have a strong sense of community, and place great value on the people in their neighborhoods as well as their family members. People in Myanmar protect one another and have an admirable resilience.

A Padaung family in Myanmar. Most families in Myanmar have two or three children.

Education

Traditionally, education in Myanmar was the responsibility of Buddhist monasteries. During British colonial times, the education system expanded dramatically. Thousands of young girls had the opportunity to gain an education for the first time. When Burma became independent from Great Britain in 1948, its new government was determined to improve educational standards for its citizens, but disorganization and a lack of money made this difficult. In recent years, however, the government has shown a renewed commitment to education. Most Burmese people now get at least a basic education, and about nine out of every ten adults in the country can read and write.

A teacher leads a class of young children at a village school in Myanmar.

Children recite lessons at a school in Shan State.

The first level of education for a Burmese child is preschool. This is followed by an elementary education that runs from kindergarten through fourth grade. In Myanmar, however, the levels are referred to as "standards" rather than "grades." Although officially the government requires all students to complete elementary school, many do not. In poor or remote areas, many children have to work to help their families survive.

Middle school includes Standards 5 through 8, and high school has Standards 9 and 10. Once in high school, Burmese students generally study either the arts or the sciences. All high school students are required to study mathematics. They also must continue taking classes in their first language, and study English, which many begin taking in their first year of

Dressing for School

Burmese students wear uniforms from elementary school all the way through high school. In elementary school, boys wear dark green pants and a white shirt. Girls wear a skirt instead of pants. The teachers sometimes dress similarly to their students. As the students grow older, they sometimes have a choice about the type of clothes they wear, but not the color scheme. For example, boys might wear a sarong instead of pants, and girls might wear a dress instead of a skirt.

elementary school. High school students who choose to study the arts will take courses in history, geography, and economics. Studying the sciences, on the other hand, will lead to courses in biology, chemistry, and physics.

A young Burmese woman studying. In recent years, a greater number of women than men have been attending university in Myanmar.

After completing high school, a student takes an exam in order to be admitted into college. Myanmar has dozens of colleges and universities along with more than a hundred vocational or technical schools offering degrees in a wide variety of subjects. Medical certification is highly desirable because it can lead to a job in Myanmar or in another country where the standard of living may be better.

Mealtime

A traditional meal in a Burmese home is usually served on a low table. Diners sit cross-legged on mats rather than in

Some people in Myanmar eat with chopsticks.

A woman cooks food
for a school. Curries are
popular dishes.

chairs. The eldest family members receive their meals first. If
they are unable to join the rest of the family, a tiny portion of
food will still be set aside for them in observance of tradition.

Typically, Burmese meals include foods such as fish, rice,
noodles, potatoes, and many fruits and vegetables. Soups are
popular and can be made using a wide variety of ingredients.
Religious customs play heavily into food choices. For example,
Buddhists generally avoid beef products, and there are times
of the year when Buddhists will adopt a fully vegetarian diet
or eat only breakfast and lunch. Surrounding nations have
also influenced Burmese cuisine. Many spices used in Burmese
cooking come from India, and several sauces and noodle varieties are of Chinese origin.

Coconut Rice

Rice is an important part of Burmese meals. Sometimes Burmese cooks serve plain white rice, and sometimes the rice is given additional flavors. Have an adult help you make this recipe for coconut rice.

Ingredients

2 cups long-grained white rice

1¼ cups water

1¾ cups coconut milk (1 can)

½ teaspoon salt

Directions

Place all ingredients in a saucepan and heat until the mixture comes to a boil. Turn the heat down to a simmer and stir. Cover with a lid and cook for about 20 minutes. Stir briefly and then cover again and cook over very low heat for another 10 minutes. Fluff with a fork. Serve with any vegetables, curries, or soup.

One of the most common food items in Myanmar is a salty paste called *ngapi* that is made from fish or shrimp. The fish or shrimp is fermented, salted, finely ground, and left to dry in the sun. There are many different uses for ngapi. It is used to season meats, prepare vegetables, and give extra flavor to soups or salads, and it is even used as a binding agent in treats. It can also serve as a condiment, be turned into a dip, or be roasted or baked and eaten on its own. Ngapi is far more common in the cuisine of southern Myanmar, but it is gradually becoming more popular in the central and northern parts of the country.

Ngapi is a salty condiment that is added to most dishes in southern Myanmar.

National Holidays

Independence Day	January 4
Union Day	February 12
Peasants' Day	March 2
Full Moon Day of Tabaung	March
Thingyan Festival	April
May Day	May 1
Full Moon Day of Kasong	May
Full Moon Day of Waso	July
Martyrs' Day	July 19
Thadingyut	October
Full Moon Day of Tasaungmone	November
National Day	November or December
Christmas	December 25

Holidays

Many of Myanmar's holidays are focused on Buddhist traditions. One of the most important is the Thadingyut Festival, the Festival of Lights, which takes place in October. It marks the end of Buddhist lent, or Vassa. Typically, during Vassa, Theravada Buddhists give up personal habits they consider barriers in their quest for nirvana, such as smoking or drinking alcohol, in the hope that they will not return to them once Vassa has concluded. Monks and other holy men may go into deep meditation during this period. During the festival, lanterns fill pagodas, and people pour into the streets to enjoy delicious food, each other's company, and theater performances.

Myanmar celebrates Independence Day on January 4, the day in 1948 when the nation officially became independent of

British rule. Myanmar also has a celebration of Burmese New Year, beginning with the Thingyan Festival in mid-April. It is a joyous festival, filled with music, floats—and a lot of water. One of the main festival activities that people take part in is dousing one another with water. The Burmese use water pistols, water balloons, pots, hoses, and anything else they can find to drench one another. It is a time to relax and have fun. Then, on New Year's Day itself, Burmese honor their elders, pray, and make resolutions for the coming year.

Children enjoy getting drenched at the Thingyan Festival.

Timeline

MYANMAR HISTORY

The British clear the Irrawaddy Delta to plant rice. — **Early 1900s**

Saya San leads a peasant uprising against the British. — **1930**

University students go on strike in opposition to British rule. — **1936**

The British give Burma its own constitution. — **1937**

The Panglong Agreement defines the borders of Myanmar. — **1947**

Myanmar becomes independent. — **1948**

U Thant becomes secretary general of the United Nations. — **1961**

Myanmar becomes socialist as the government takes control of most businesses. — **1962**

Military leaders brutally suppress widespread protests, killing thousands. — **1988**

Aung San Suu Kyi wins the Nobel Peace Prize for her pro-democracy efforts. — **1991**

Myanmar enacts a new constitution. — **2008**

Thein Sein becomes president of Myanmar. — **2011**

The National League for Democracy wins a landslide election, giving it control of the government. — **2015**

WORLD HISTORY

1914 — World War I begins.

1917 — The Bolshevik Revolution brings communism to Russia.

1929 — A worldwide economic depression begins.

1939 — World War II begins.

1945 — World War II ends.

1969 — Humans land on the Moon.

1975 — The Vietnam War ends.

1989 — The Berlin Wall is torn down as communism crumbles in Eastern Europe.

1991 — The Soviet Union breaks into separate states.

2001 — Terrorists attack the World Trade Center in New York City and the Pentagon near Washington, D.C.

2004 — A tsunami in the Indian Ocean destroys coastlines in Africa, India, and Southeast Asia.

2008 — The United States elects its first African American president.

Fast Facts

Official name: Republic of the Union of Myanmar

Capital: Nay Pyi Taw

Year of founding: 1948

Yangon

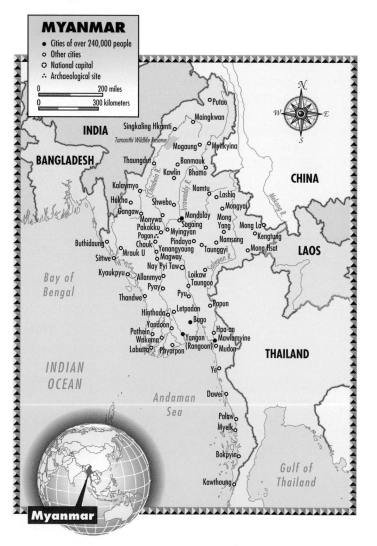

National flag

National anthem:	"Kaba Ma Kyei" ("Till the End of the World")
Official language:	Burmese
Official religion:	None
Type of government:	Constitutional republic
Head of state:	President
Head of government:	President
Bordering countries:	India and Bangladesh to the west, China to the northeast, Laos and Thailand to the east
Latitude and longitude of capital city:	19.4° N, 96.1° E
Area:	About 261,000 square miles (676,000 sq km)
Highest elevation:	Mount Hkakabo, 19,296 feet (5,881 m)
Lowest elevation:	Sea level along the coast
Longest river:	Irrawaddy, about 1,350 miles (2,200 km)
Longest border:	With Thailand, 1,501 miles (2,416 km)
Average high temperature:	In Yangon, 99°F (37°C) in April; 89°F (32°C) in October
Average low temperature:	In Yangon, 76°F (24°C) in April; 76°F (24°C) in October
Average annual precipitation:	In Yangon, 106 inches (269 cm)

Mount Hkakabo

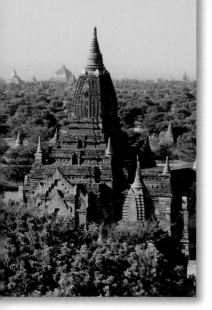

Pagan

Currency

National population (2014 est.):	51,419,420	

Population of major cities (2015 est.):

Yangon	4,477,638
Mandalay	1,208,099
Nay Pyi Taw	925,000
Mawlamyine	438,861
Bago	244,376

Landmarks:
- ▶ *Mergui Archipelago*, southwestern coast
- ▶ *Pagan*, Mandalay region
- ▶ *Pindaya Caves*, Pindaya
- ▶ *Shwedagon Pagoda*, Yangon
- ▶ *U Thant House*, Yangon

Economy: Most Burmese work in agriculture. Rice is the most important crop. Other major crops include beans, peanuts, sugarcane, and rubber. Fishing and logging are important industries. Teak is the most important wood. Myanmar is one of the world's leading producers of gemstones, mining large quantities of rubies and sapphires. Copper mining and oil and gas drilling are also important industries. Products manufactured in Myanmar include cigarettes, cement, steel, and textiles.

Currency: The kyat. In 2015, US$1.00 equaled about 1,280 kyat.

System of weights and measures: A mixture of traditional Burmese units, imperial units, and the metric system

Literacy rate: 89.5%

Students

Aung San Suu Kyi

Common Burmese words and phrases:

Min-ga-la-ba	Hello
Kamya ne-kaun-la?	How are you?
Kamya ne-meh beh-lo k'aw-leh?	What's your name?
Sain bhaalkalell?	Where are you from?
Kan-kaung-ba-zay	Good luck
Shin aaingaliutlo pyaw lar?	Do you speak English?
Ce-zu tin-bah-deh	Thank you
Bhine	Good-bye

Prominent Burmese people:

Anawrahta (1014–1077)
The first king of Burma

Aung San Suu Kyi (1945–)
Political activist

Saya San (1876–1931)
Leader in the fight against colonialism

Thakin Kodaw Hmaing (1876–1964)
Writer

U Ne Win (1911–2002)
Military commander and prime minister

U Thant (1909–1974)
Politician and diplomat

To Find Out More

Books

▶ Berlatsky, Noah (editor). *Burma.* Farmington Hills, MI: Greenhaven Press, 2015.

▶ DK Publishing. *Travel Guide: Myanmar (Burma).* London: DK Eyewitness Travel, 2014.

▶ LaBella, Laura. *Aung San Suu Kyi: Myanmar's Freedom Fighter.* New York: Rosen, 2014.

▶ Steinberg, David I. *Burma/ Myanmar: What Everyone Needs to Know.* New York: Oxford University Press, 2013.

▶ Yin, Myat Saw, and Josie Elias. *Myanmar.* New York: Cavendish Square, 2012.

Music

▶ *Burma: Traditional Music.* Boulogne, France: Playasound, 2008.

▶ *Mahagita: Harp and Vocal Music of Burma.* Washington, DC: Smithsonian Folkways, 2003.

▶ Visit this Scholastic Web site for more information on Myanmar:
www.factsfornow.scholastic.com
Enter the keyword **Myanmar**

Index

Page numbers in *italics*
indicate illustrations.

Meet the Author

WIL MARA IS THE AWARD-WINNING author of more than 140 books, many of them educational titles for children in Scholastic's catalog. He began writing in the late 1980s with several nonfiction titles about herpetology. He branched out into fiction in the mid-1990s, when he ghostwrote five of the popular Boxcar Children Mysteries. He has since authored more than a dozen novels, including *Wave*, which was a recipient of the 2005 New Jersey Notable Book Award, *The Gemini Virus*, and the *New York Times* best seller *Frame 232*, which reached the number one spot in its category on Amazon .com and won the 2013 Lime Award for Excellence in Fiction.

Photo Credits